CHI

LAKOTA HOOP DANCER

Text by
Jacqueline Left Hand Bull
and **Suzanne Haldane**

With Photographs by
Suzanne Haldane

Dutton Children's Books
New York

Kevin Locke and Jacqueline Left Hand Bull prefer to be called Lakota rather than Sioux, and American Indian rather than Native American. Lakota people have long called themselves Lakota; Sioux is a name given to them by others. American Indian is the term that refers to the various nations in North America that made treaties with the U.S. government. These treaties are still in effect. It is also the designation used in a particular spiritual prophecy close to the heart of both Kevin and Jacqueline.

ACKNOWLEDGMENTS

We would like to thank the following people for their help in the making of this book:
Nancy Cayford; Mary Davis, Huntington Free Library, Bronx, New York; Jim Deerhawk; Tom Galliher;
Gail Grainger; Katherine Hyman; Victoria Laird; Kevin Locke and his family, particularly Patricia Locke;
the people of Little Eagle, South Dakota; the people of Wakpala, South Dakota; Dale Weasel and
The Running Antelope Drum; Bruce Wendt; and Francis Whitebird.

Text copyright © 1999 by Jacqueline Left Hand Bull and Suzanne Haldane
Photographs of the sun/moon, butterfly, eagle, and hoop of many hoops designs
on pages 27–29 copyright © 1999 by Tom Galliher
All other photographs copyright © 1999 by Suzanne Haldane
All rights reserved.
Library of Congress Cataloging-in-Publication Data
Left Hand Bull, Jacqueline.
Lakota hoop dancer/ text by Jacqueline Left Hand Bull
and Suzanne Haldane; photographs by Suzanne Haldane.—1st ed.   p.   cm.
Summary: Follows the activities of Kevin Locke, a Hunkpapa Indian, as he prepares for and performs the traditional Lakota hoop dance.
ISBN 0-525-45413-6 (hc)
1. Teton Indians—Juvenile literature. 2. Hoop dance—South Dakota—Juvenile literature.
[1. Hoop dance. 2. Teton Indians. 3. Indians of North America—South Dakota] I. Haldane, Suzanne, ill. II. Title.
E99.T34L43   1999   793.3'19783'0899752—dc21   98-21905   CIP   AC
Published in the United States 1999 by Dutton Children's Books,
a division of Penguin Putnam Books for Young Readers
345 Hudson Street, New York, New York 10014
http://www.penguinputnam.com/yreaders/index.htm
Designed by Ellen M. Lucaire
Printed in Hong Kong   First Edition
1 3 5 7 9 10 8 6 4 2

Sincaŋǧu Oyate nahaŋ wakaŋyeja—
tona wetu wakaŋ wicayalapi nahaŋ tena caŋgleška
wakaŋ ayapiyapi nahaŋ tona oyate waŋjila yakagapi—
lecacicicoŋpikšto.

Rosebud people, young people—
those who believe in the spiritual springtime, who are
mending the sacred hoop and are making the nations one—
for all of you, I do this.
—J.L.H.B.

For my parents, Nona and Bill Haldane,
and my mother-in-law, Bernice Hyman,
and for Ian—in his tenth year
—S.H.

LAKOTA HOMELAND

Repeated strikes on the drum—like a heart-beat—and an intense, chantlike song draw people near. In the still, stubborn heat of a summer's day, an American Indian man performs a breathtaking dance for an eager audience. Red, yellow, and blue colors blur. His braided hair and the fringe on his outfit sway and snap. Hoops whirl.

People from many Indian Nations perform the hoop dance. No one knows for certain when or how the dance began. However, paintings of Lakota people dancing with hoops were made in the 1700s, and the dance was the subject of traditional Lakota songs that were recorded in the early 1900s. At that time, the hoop dance was called the rainbow dance.

Now this present-day hoop dancer is performing on an outdoor stage in the New England mill town of Lowell, Massachusetts—far, far from the place where he lives.

Kevin Locke, whose Indian name is Tokeya Inajin (translated into English as "Stands First"), is a member of the Lakota Nation. He lives in a small *tiošpaye* on the Standing Rock Reservation, in north central South Dakota. A *tiošpaye* is a family or clan that includes parents, children, cousins, aunts, uncles, and grandparents. Such an extended family is very important to Lakota people. They believe it is good to have children grow up guided by the love and wisdom of their many relatives. Kevin Locke's three children grew up in a *tiošpaye*. Long ago, extended families each had their own special place in the camp circle.

The land is wide open in Kevin's part of the country. Trees grow mostly in ravines and along the rivers. Vast stretches of the landscape may be dotted with cattle or bison—but not buildings.

Although Kevin has visited many countries, no other place pleases him as much as the land his family calls home. After his performances at the Lowell Folk Festival, it was only a matter of hours before he was on an airplane heading back there.

"The state of South Dakota covers an area that was only a part of my ancestral home," he says. "My family lives on land that has been occupied by people for perhaps as many as twelve thousand years. Descendants of those early people live here, doing many of the things we have done for generations.

"We are Hunkpapa, one of the tribal groups of the Lakota Nation. Sitting Bull (Tatankiyotake) was one of our well-known Hunkpapa leaders. People say he was born, and died, near here.

"My home is on the plains. When I'm away from here, I miss the far-stretching vistas, the thunder, the cool early-morning songs of the meadowlark. I miss the smell of the sage and the wild, roadside sunflowers. I look forward to picking enough chokecherries to dry. All year we make *wojapi*, a kind of pudding, from the dried chokecherry patties.

"It's good to swim in the river with the kids and to visit with people from all the little communities on the reservation. Of course, it gets kind of cold in the winter here!"

His family's houses are on the bluff overlooking the place where the Missouri and Grand rivers meet. It is fitting for him to live at the junction of two rivers, for he sees himself as the joiner of two cultures—of all cultures, he would even say. Lakota people finish their prayers with the phrase *"Mitakuye oyasin"*—*"We are all related"*—to include all people and all living things everywhere in the blessings of the prayers just offered.

From the houses on the bluff Kevin can see beyond the reservation. To the northwest is the reservation town of Wakpala. To the east and across the Missouri River is the non-reservation town of Mobridge, South Dakota. The view reminds him of the world beyond his family, community, and nation. If he stands in one spot and slowly turns in a full circle, he can see a distant horizon in each direction. It is like looking at a hoop where the earth meets the sky all around him. Inside that hoop is the prairie, full of life. Kevin says it is a hoop of life.

Keeping Lakota Culture Alive

Kevin Locke is committed to preserving the beauty of his culture without turning his back on the rest of the world. He wants to do his part to keep Lakota traditions alive.

"My uncle and others of his generation would often need a driver or companion to go on trips to various events. He would get some money and say, 'Let's buy some gas and go visiting.' So on these trips with those older men, I would learn a lot by just listening and observing. Of course, one learns the culture one lives in every day in many ways."

In the same way that Kevin's uncles nurtured his love for Lakota culture, Kevin often takes at least one of his children with him when he travels to perform his dances. Sometimes he takes their friends along as well. This has proved a good way to teach his own children dancing skills and other cultural values, and to spend time with them.

In addition to hoop dancing, singing, and learning three dialects of the Lakota language, Kevin has collected and recorded Northern Plains flute music and stories. The Lakota consider the flute an instrument of enchantment and courtship. Long ago, young men used specially composed melodies to lure and win the hearts of the young women they hoped to marry.

Kevin plays his handcrafted cedarwood flute for audiences, friends, and family. When his younger daughter was little, the music from his flute, like a lullaby, coaxed her to sleep.

Kevin has always been interested in music and dance. He and members of his family dance at powwows. The powwow is a social gathering where Indians meet to share fun, to dance, and to visit with old and new friends. There is food, a ceremony honoring United States military veterans, dance competitions, and special programs. The main part of the powwow is always the *wacipi,* the dancing.

When Kevin goes to powwows, he dances as long as time allows. He says, "If I couldn't dance, I don't know what I'd do."

As a youngster, he was fascinated by the hoop dance from the moment he first saw it performed. But it was not until he was a young man that he learned how the dance was done and what traditions lay behind it.

The hoop dance requires the skills of an athlete and the timing of a juggler. Few dancers are willing to put in the effort necessary to learn it. Although the dance is usually done as a solo exhibition at powwows or in theaters, some powwows do have hoop-dance competitions.

Arlo Goodbear, a Mandan-Hidatsa hoop dancer from North Dakota, wanted to teach Kevin how to dance with hoops. They met each other at an event in New York City. That evening Arlo gave Kevin his first lesson, showing him what the basic steps were and how to hold the hoops.

They parted with the intention of meeting again for more lessons. But that was the last time they were together; Arlo died soon after that New York trip.

It was up to Kevin to remember what he had been taught. He says, "After his death, Arlo would be in my dreams dancing with hoops. I felt that the dreams were encouraging me to become a hoop dancer. A few months later I had a chance to tour Africa, and I decided to put together a hoop-dance presentation."

His first exhibition was in the country of Senegal, Africa. He took part in a cultural arts tour sponsored by the U.S. Department of State.

"When we got to Senegal, we had three days to rest before our first performance. I went to an empty gym in a school. I began to practice and I remembered Arlo dancing. I imitated what he did in my memory of him. I practiced until I could give a good demonstration with about twelve hoops. That was my first hoop-dance performance for an audience. Since then I have been adding new moves, always trying to improve. I'm still learning how to apply new ideas."

THE HOOP

The hoop, or circle, is an important symbol for all American Indian people. It signifies unity, equality, harmony, and balance. It also symbolizes the cycles of life, the yearly renewal that comes as the seasons change. Today it brings to mind our round planet and all that we as humans share on Earth. Black Elk, a Lakota holy man who lived from about 1863 to 1950, told of a vision he had. In it, he saw a time of prosperity and well-being for the people—people who were gathered in a large hoop made up of many hoops. These many hoops represented groups or nations of people, living together in harmony.

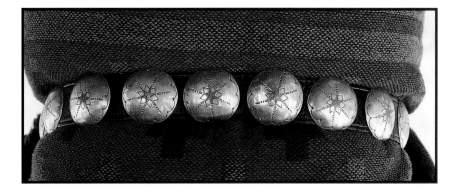

The hoop, or circle, can be found throughout American Indian life. The base of a tipi is a circle. During religious ceremonies, social meetings, and dances, Indian people gather in a circle. For example, the traditional arena in which a powwow takes place is a circle. And the hoop is a frequent design element in Indian arts and crafts.

Kevin tells his audiences, "When people gather in a circle, everyone is equal and no one is left out."

KEVIN'S HOOPS

As people do in all cultures, Indians adopt customs, including dance customs, from one another. Each dancer interprets the hoop dance in a unique way. Kevin Locke uses twenty-eight hoops in his version of the dance; this number represents the twenty-eight days of the moon's cycle.

He makes each hoop exactly the way he wants it. All twenty-eight hoops have a diameter of about twenty-eight inches—roughly twice the size of a basketball hoop or about the diameter of a car tire, and just a few inches wider than the width of Kevin's shoulders. That's a surprisingly small area, since he must slip many hoops at once over parts of his body with swiftness and accuracy. He makes many designs with the hoops, changing from one to another, while he dances to the music of Indian songs.

Not all hoops are fashioned from the same material. In earlier times, hoops were made from willow branches. When Kevin began hoop dancing, he, too, made his hoops from willow. But now he uses rattan for sixteen of his hoops and plastic tubing for twelve others. Rattan is a kind of long vine that is very strong. When the center is scooped out, it is like a long tube. Rattan and plastic are more durable than willow. They can withstand the rigors of Kevin's performances.

To make a rattan hoop, Kevin takes a piece of rattan to the river and places it in the water. In a few hours, it becomes flexible enough to bend. When it's pliable, he forms the rattan until he has the correct diameter. Then he cuts off the excess, if necessary, and binds the ends together with tape.

His use of plastic tubing for hoops came about in a surprising way. Once, when Kevin was traveling in Australia, the airline baggage handlers accidentally crushed his rattan hoops. The hoops were totally destroyed, and he had a performance scheduled. There was no time to find rattan and make new hoops.

To get ideas, he went to a hardware store. There he found some flexible plastic tubing and wooden dowels. He cut the tubing to the desired length. Then he inserted a small piece of dowel into each end to make a strong wooden joint with an even alignment. Next he taped the seam. Finally he wrapped the whole hoop with colored tape.

Kevin still uses those same twelve hoops made in a hurry years ago. These days, almost all hoop dancers use plastic tubing for their hoops. It is heavier than rattan and willow but has extra flexibility.

Kevin's hoops are white, red, yellow, and black—

significant colors in Lakota tradition. They are the colors of the four directions (north, east, south, and west). Some American Indians say they are the colors of the four races of human-kind.

Kevin wraps each hoop with plastic tape in one of the four colors. This protects the hoops without interfering with their flexibility. Now his hoops are ready to be used for dancing. He has also made fifty extra hoops to take with him when he travels. He uses these hoops to let the children in his audiences try a few simple steps and designs.

Kevin carries all his hoops in a beautifully decorated round canvas case made especially for them.

THE REGALIA

Preparing hoops is just one part of getting ready for the hoop dance. Designing and making an outfit is an important step, too. The outfit is sometimes referred to as *regalia*. A person's regalia is often said to be a personal statement, even a kind of biography. The various pieces of a dance outfit reflect the tribe's traditional dress and the dance for which it is intended. Some dancers have pieces passed down from family members. The many pieces of Kevin's regalia have been specially made for him by family or friends. Whatever the source, each piece represents many hours of work and a great deal of love and respect.

Tiny glass beads (called seed beads), colored ribbons, bells, feathers, and other materials are stitched in traditional patterns to the fabric of the garment. The seed beads, which are the size of pinheads, and other decorations must be sewn on by hand. Only the ribbons are sewn to the cloth with a sewing machine.

Traditional Lakota dress is usually decorated with designs that are geometric. Indians from other regions of America use different design forms. For example, traditional designs used by tribes from the East and Midwest feature floral elements.

Kevin often gives dance performances at schools and other places that have smooth, polished floors. The stiff leather sole of a traditional moccasin could cause him to slip on such surfaces. So Kevin had his local shoe-repair shop add rubber soles to his moccasins. He combines traditional and contemporary materials to make certain he has sure footing.

apron

cape used for grass dancing

When a dancer begins to put together a dance outfit, he or she must know what kind of dance will be performed.

Kevin Locke is a grass dancer as well as a hoop dancer. Grass dancing is a traditional Northern Plains dance that imitates the beautiful and life-giving tall buffalo grass of the prairie. This grass, which waves and ripples in a breeze, is almost extinct now. In all of North America, only a few protected patches are left. The regalia for the grass dance includes a cape and an apron with long fringe that sways like grass to the movements of the dance.

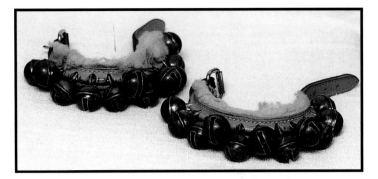

ankle bells

ankle fringe

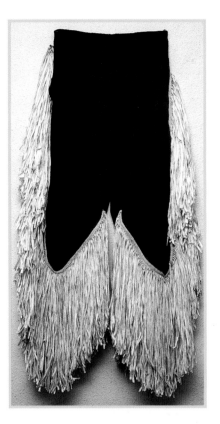

fringed leggings
for grass dancing

In addition to a cape and an apron, Kevin wears a headdress called a roach. It is made of guard hair from the sides of the porcupine and hair from the tail of the white-tailed deer. Two eagle feathers top the roach at the crown. Kevin also wears a beaded harness, belt, gauntlets at his wrist, heavily fringed leggings, anklets, ankle bells, and beaded moccasins.

For hoop dancing, Kevin doesn't wear the cape, because the long fringe would tangle in the hoops. Instead, he wears a shirt decorated with ribbons. He doesn't wear the roach with the eagle feathers, either, because it would brush or catch on the hoops as he slips through them. Instead, he wears a wide headband, beaded with the same design as his belt and moccasins. His headband helps to keep his hair out of his eyes as he whirls and bends.

Kevin composed the designs on his regalia. He asked a Canadian Indian man, known for the excellence of his beadwork, to sew the beaded parts of his outfit. The designs include the four traditional Lakota colors.

Complete dance outfits sometimes weigh as much as forty or fifty pounds. The dancers often dance for many hours with little rest. To do that and look light on his or her feet and to show spirit in performing each dance, the dancer must also be an athlete. On days that he doesn't dance, Kevin runs several miles to keep in good condition.

THE SONGS

Dancers everywhere respond to good dance rhythms. The rhythm of American Indian music is made by the singers at the drum. Although their song is accompanied by a simple drumbeat, the dance rhythm is created by the song's changing tones and melody and by the way the singers repeat phrases. To be considered a good drum group, the singers must understand all the parts that make the complex rhythm.

Singers begin a song several phrases before the drum begins, and they may continue singing after the last drumbeat. In some dances, a dancer is expected to stop exactly at the last drumbeat.

An Indian drum group is usually made up of at least five men. Sometimes women stand behind the men sitting at the drum and sing with them. Each group has a lead singer who guides the song, watches the dancers, and determines how long the song will be. The singers practice many hours together to get the best sound. They may learn several hundred songs, changing them to suit the occasion and their own taste.

Northern Plains songs require singers to sing notes that are in a high range, known as falsetto. The "false" high pitch puts a strain on their voices. To give singers a rest, several drum groups take turns singing for dancers; or sometimes audiotapes are played.

A hoop dance requires a song with a steady rhythm. Kevin tells the singers what he needs, and they choose the best song for his dance.

Many places Kevin visits have no Indian drum groups to sing for him. So he always takes along a few favorite tapes or compact discs of Indian music that he knows are good for hoop dancing. He also knows hundreds of songs himself. When he is not dancing, he can sit with a drum group to help sing.

THE DANCE

Kevin Locke's performance of the hoop dance is far more than a display of beautiful regalia. And it is more than a demonstration of skill. Through his dance, Kevin conveys a message of hope for the future. He proclaims the continuity of the cycle of life. He tells a story of springtime. He captures a timelessness, bridging past and present, present and future. His dance praises the physical world of the here and now, but also the unseen world around us. It draws a circle that includes everybody. It celebrates the nobility of the human spirit.

Kevin does all this with an astonishing, whirling, nonstop rhythmic energy. Fringe flies outward as knees lift. Moccasins seem to barely touch the floor. Dark arms raise hoops higher. Fingers deftly change the hoop patterns. Sometimes Kevin needs to hold a hoop by his teeth to complete a design.

His foot taps, and hoops quickly roll upward to be added to the mix. Suddenly there is a moon, a butterfly, a rainbow, an eagle.

But Kevin also takes time to tell the audience about the designs he makes. He begins by explaining that the sun and the moon designs show us that at the start of each day we, too, have a chance to awaken and begin afresh. The designs also tell us of the blessings we all receive each new day. He says that we can see the sun and the moon in his dance and realize our connection to one another.

He makes flowers to remind us of new plants in the spring. Every day there is a new bird singing, a new flower opening to bloom. Lilac, pineberry, plum, and chokecherry blossoms come forth one after another. Each wafts its fragrance into the spring air.

Butterfly

Sun/Moon

Eagle

He makes a bird design in the dance and explains that our spirits are like the bird. This is our day to soar. We are the eagles.

He takes twelve hoops and fashions them into a series of interlinked hoops. He lays them down to make a road—a new road to travel. He picks the road up in the middle and it becomes a bridge—

a bridge to help us pass over obstacles: racism, anger, ignorance.

Kevin holds the interlinked hoops vertically. Now they form a ladder, taking us to new heights in helping all people.

Next he holds the hoops as though they were wings—wings that allow us to soar.

Then he hooks the interlinked hoops into a hoop of many hoops. He tells how these hoops represent groups and nations of people living interlinked in harmony and prosperity. Our privilege is to work to make that happen. Black Elk saw all this in his vision many decades ago. We see it coming true in our time.

Kevin makes a hoop of many hoops to show the strength of togetherness. When one hoop is taken out, the whole structure collapses. This understanding of a global community is growing all over the world.

His audience may be in the Russian Arctic or in Brazil; in Turkey or on islands in the Pacific; in Lowell, Massachusetts, or in Wakpala, South Dakota. As Kevin holds the sphere of hoops above his head, he shows the audience that they too are part of the hoop of many hoops.

All this is Kevin Locke's hoop dance.

The Fun

American Indian children learn to dance almost as soon as they can walk. In full regalia, kids as young as three or four years old participate in pow-wows. Often they take part in dance competitions in their age category—Tiny Tots.

Until recently, the hoop dance was performed only by men. Today young women have begun to spin through the hoops. Kevin teaches the children of his community how to whirl the hoops while dancing a step they already know well.

Recorded songs provide the rhythm. Each student practices with four or five hoops. It isn't easy. Hoops slip, spill, and roll. But with practice come success and a smile!

Perhaps one of these children will become another Lakota hoop dancer. If so, it would be in keeping with what Kevin Locke often tells his audiences: "I dedicate this dance to each and every one of you, to the nobility of the eagle in each of you—in each of us!"

GLOSSARY

Black Elk an Oglala Lakota man who lived from 1863(?) to 1950 and whose visions as described to John Niehardt have inspired many people

chokecherry a wild cherry that Lakota people use to make a favorite pudding called *wojapi*

the drum a term that often refers to the group of people who sit around a large drum and beat a rhythm on the drum to accompany the songs they sing

eagle feather the most sacred feather to most American Indians. The eagle's flight represents the spirit, courage, and power of human beings to rise above their selfish "lower" nature. Sometimes people honor a person's efforts by presenting them with an eagle feather.

Lakota Nation a nation of people, made up of seven major tribes, who speak a common language known as Lakota and whose homelands are the northern plains of the United States and the western plains of Canada. Lakota means "the people who live in harmony."

Mitakuye oyasin (me-dock-oo-yay oh-yah-see) a Lakota sentence generally spoken as a prayer for all of one's relatives, indicating that the one who is praying considers all living things to be related to him or her

powwow a social gathering where people come together for traditional dancing, to share food, to meet relatives and old friends, and to make new friends. Sometimes other activities, such as storytelling contests, races, honoring ceremonies, and handicraft sales, are included.

regalia a dancer's clothing, headdress, and other adornments

roach a headdress worn by male dancers in several kinds of dances. It is usually made from porcupine guard hair or stiff deer hair, with two eagle feathers in the middle of the top.

tiošpaye (tee-osh-pa-yay) a Lakota word meaning "extended family or clan"—parents, children, grandparents, uncles and aunts, cousins, second cousins, great-aunts and great-uncles, and relatives by marriage and adoption

vision an experience of seeing, while awake, unusual things as though in a dream. The things seen in a vision often tell the person about his or her life and the lives of loved ones. Some visions tell the future.

wacipi (wah-chee-pee) a Lakota word that means "to dance" or "a dance" or "people dancing"

wojapi (wo-zhah-pee) the Lakota name for a delicious sweet pudding made from dried chokecherries, sugar, and a small amount of flour or cornstarch mixed with water

RECOMMENDED READING

Driving Hawk Sneve, Virginia, and Ronald Himler. *The Sioux: A First Americans Book*. New York: Holiday House, 1993.

Goble, Paul. *Love Flute*. New York: Simon and Schuster Books for Young Readers, 1992. (Paul Goble has written many other books, including the Plains Indian Stories about Itomi.)

Neihardt, John G. *Black Elk Speaks*. Lincoln, Nebr.: University of Nebraska Press, 1932; reprint, 1972.

Rubalcaba, Jill, and Irving Toddy. *Uncegila's Seventh Spot: A Lakota Legend*. New York: Clarion Books, 1995.

Standing Bear, Luther. *Land of the Spotted Eagle*. Lincoln, Nebr.: University of Nebraska Press, 1933.

———. *My Indian Boyhood*. Lincoln, Nebr.: University of Nebraska Press, 1931.